# I.T. WORKS

*An Information and Communication Technology programme for the Primary Years*

# Teacher Resource
# for Nursery/Reception/P1

# Contents

Introduction ........................................................................................ 2

I.C.T. in the Early Years ..................................................................... 3

General Technological Awareness ........................................... 5

Paint, Draw and Graphics ........................................................ 12

Word Processing ......................................................................... 14

Keyboarding ............................................................................... 27

Control ......................................................................................... 33

Video ............................................................................................ 46

Information Handling ................................................................. 49

Skill Matrices .................................................................................... 61

Assessing I.C.T. Skills ....................................................................... 63

Record Sheet .................................................................................... 64

© Teacher Created Materials/Folens
This edition is published by arrangement with Teacher Created Materials

# Introduction

*I.T. Works* provides a comprehensive **information** and **communication technology** course for children aged 4–11. The logical way to teach *I.T. Works* lessons is to begin with the first section and work sequentially through the book. However, *I.T. Works* is also designed so that each section is self-contained enabling teachers to adapt it to their particular situation. For example, a Science or Geography topic may lend itself to the use of a database program, in which case the Information Handling section could be covered as part of the topic.

*I.T. Works* contains three elements:
- Activity Cards
- Teacher Resource Books
- Co-ordinator's Manuals.

This Nursery/Reception/P1 Book combines the Activity Cards and Teacher Resource Book, replacing cards with ideas for activities to be completed with the children. Photocopiable resources are also provided.

## Activities

The activities introduce young children to key I.C.T. skills which are developed using the Activity Cards throughout the *I.T. Works* programme. The activities in this introductory book are designed to be carried out initially with an adult but also provide opportunities for children to work independently, where appropriate. The Activity Cards in Units 1-6 are designed to be self-directed so that children can complete the tasks independently. Icons are used alongside the text to assist early readers. This system is also useful for children for whom English is an additional language.

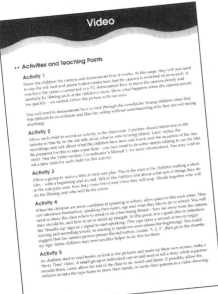

## Teacher Resource Books

Units 1–6 are accompanied by separate Teacher Resource Books. The Nursery/Reception/P1 Book incorporates elements of these books. Each book contains:

- **Lesson Support Plans** – these are designed to provide support to the teacher in introducing new knowledge and skills. Each lesson plan is linked to a single or a group of activities (or Activity Cards in Units 1–6). Each contains the learning objectives; a list of materials needed; important teaching points, including ideas for introductory or follow up work; and target vocabulary.
- **Photocopiable Resources** – these relate directly to the classroom activities being proposed.
- **Pupil Record Sheets** – these are linked to all the activities children encounter in a year.

## Co-ordinator's Manuals

There are two manuals: one covering the content for ages 4–7 and one for ages 7–11. The manuals provide a high level of support for the I.C.T. co-ordinators in schools. They include all the technical guidance needed for effective I.C.T. – explanations of technical language; support for constructing a school policy and scheme of work; and photocopiable certificates for pupil achievement.

# I.C.T. in the Early Years

Time spent in Nursery, Reception and P1 is very important since this is where the foundations are laid. Many of the elements required to be competent in the use of I.C.T. will be seen in children even at this very early age.

- The ability to ask questions, to explore for themselves, to test things out and to look for solutions.
- Children begin to develop and refine their communication skills and creativity in a variety of activities. They gain increasing self-control and independence.
- Activities where children are encouraged to match and sort, and to look for similarities and differences form the basis of all information handling.
- Children's sense of number, size, shape and space is also developed though rhymes, games, movement and play.

It is important to introduce children to I.C.T. as early as possible because it plays an increasingly important role in education and the world around us. The use of I.C.T. can develop and support a wide range of learning activities. It can encourage such varied elements as developing positive attitudes to errors, modelling of aspects of the real world through role-play, and supporting early literacy and numeracy skills.

Many activities in Nursery, Reception and P1 classes are centred around children developing an understanding of their environment. Most children are naturally inquisitive about all forms of technology, including the telephone, programmable toys, televisions and computers. As their awareness and understanding increase, they will begin to ask questions and try to look for similarities and differences between objects and people. Activities can guide the children in their understanding and use of the technology in the world around them – through role-play, sorting activities, class visits. Suggested activities are provided in the **General Technological Awareness** section of this book (see pages 5–7).

I.C.T. includes a wide range of resources such as programmable toys, musical keyboards, radio-controlled toys, talking toys, camcorders, etc. There are also many instances in real life where the children will experience computer control of everyday items – in the supermarket, the garage forecourt, alarm systems, automatic doors. Programmable toys, such as floor robots (Turtles, Pips, Pixies and Roamers), can be of great use to children of this early age and are great fun to use. As well as helping young children to develop spatial awareness, they can also help in the acquisition of number, distance, angle of turn and estimation skills. Children are encouraged to plan together and to think logically and sequentially. As well as this, the programmable toys work independently of any computer and so they do not 'tie up' more costly resources. Activities can be found in the **Control** section of this book (see pages 33–38).

# I.C.T. in the Early Years

One of the biggest obstacles to the acquisition of computer skills, for children and adults alike, is that computers, for the present at least, need a keyboard to input information or commands. *I.T. Works* tackles this in its section on **Keyboarding** skills which runs right through the programme. Learning letters and letter groups is also an important part of early years' learning, so awareness of the computer keyboard can also be encouraged. Ideas for using alternative devices such as overlay keyboards is also provided. At this early stage of letter recognition and the beginnings of emergent writing in the Reception Year (P1), overlay keyboards can be linked to **Word Processing** programs. Therefore, ideas are included together with photocopiable overlays (see pages 14–26).

Sorting, classifying and matching activities are already established in early years' classes. These form the basis of all information handling which is one of the most common uses of I.C.T. today. Suggestions for linking these types of activities with I.C.T., together with photocopiable activity and data collection sheets, are provided in the **Information Handling** section (see pages 49–60).

One of the important aims of the early years' curriculum is to develop and refine the children's communication skills, self-control and independence. Use of a camcorder can enhance activities, such as role-play, already taking place in the classroom. Tips and suggestions are provided in the **Video** section (see pages 46–48), an important part of the *I.T. Works* programme for developing communication skills in this TV age.

There are always lots of creative activities taking place in Nursery, Reception and P1 rooms at any time of the day. The **Paint, Draw and Graphics** section provides further support, or development for such activities (see pages 12–13). I.C.T. can not only help with the creativity of the child but also can be an important tool for the development of fine motor skills.

## Computer Software

There is now an increasing variety of software programs and CD-ROMs applicable to early years' education. Computer programs are available which can help young children to develop their literacy, numeracy and creativity. Different activities can foster their independent learning as well as their social skills.

There are programs which can enhance learning and understanding of number, counting, the alphabet, graphics, spelling, painting, shapes, matching, patterns, reading and stories – incorporating many of these activities to develop basic numeracy and literacy skills, as well as developing keyboarding skills, spatial awareness and hand/eye co-ordination.

Children today live in a 'multimedia' world and so even very young children require computer programs to be bright, cheerful and easy to access if they are to remain interested. Many of the modern 'Talking Stories' achieve this. They often contain follow-up activities to the story, or can simply be enjoyed as a story.

## •• Learning Objectives

The child can:
- understand what a computer is
- identify the parts of a computer
- explain the basics of how a computer operates
- start, restart and shutdown a computer
- understand that appliances need to be switched on and off
- understand the dos and don'ts of using a computer
- demonstrate appropriate behaviour at the computer
- treat equipment and disks with respect
- identify a mouse and explain what it does
- move a mouse and point it to a desired location.

## •• Materials

A computer, printer, disks, CDs, mouse, overlay keyboard
General equipment (or toys) demonstrating use of computer technology – keyboards, cooker, tape recorder, CD player, etc.
Photocopiable sheets – Jigsaw and Computer Parts (see pages 9 and 10)
Photocopiable sheet – On and Off (page 8)

## •• Teacher Information

The aim of this section of activities is to familiarise the children with the parts of the computer and what they do and to encourage children to look after the equipment. For detailed information on the parts of a computer, see the General Technological Awareness section, Co-ordinator's Manual 1 (Ages 4–7).

## •• Activities and Teaching Points

### Activity 1

Begin by explaining the computer to the children – that it is made of different parts which work together. It is important to introduce the children to the correct vocabulary at an early age. This is reinforced in further Units.

Make labels for the different parts, laminate them and use Blu-tak to fix them to the computer parts. Play a game with the children – read a label and ask a child to place it on the matching part. The photocopiable picture of computer parts (see page 10) can be enlarged and used for this activity. This can be kept on display near the computer with the parts labelled.

## Activity 2

Photocopy and colour the jigsaw of computer parts (see page 9). Stick this on card and laminate. This can now be cut to make a jigsaw. You may wish to make several copies of this. Children can work individually or in pairs to put the computer back together again. More able children can attempt to match labels to the completed picture, using the classroom computer (labelled) as reference.

## Activity 3

Demonstrate how to switch on the computer at the socket, and how to switch on all the parts. Ask the children to watch for lights to appear as the parts begin to work, and to listen closely for the sounds which can be heard. (Choose children in rota each day to switch on the computer correctly whilst others are observing – this can be an assessment activity).

At this stage it is doubtful whether you would introduce the children to switching off the computer (especially if you are using a Windows operating system). This is best left until the children have good control of the mouse. However, you must stress that the children cannot just switch off the equipment at the wall.

## Activity 4

Discuss with the children what other things in the classroom can be switched on and off. Ask the children to point them out and to show you where the switches are. You may choose children to operate some of them. Some children may realise that some equipment needs to be plugged into the wall, whilst other equipment uses batteries for power.

## Activity 5

Talk about items at home which need to be switched on before they work. Show the children the photocopiable sheet of appliances (On and Off – see page 8). This can be used in various ways, depending upon the ability of the children. Some children can be given the sheet, so that a cross or circle of one colour can be placed over items found at home and another colour can be used for items found in school. For other children, stick a sheet onto card, laminate it, then cut up the pictures and use as a sorting activity.

## Activity 6

Use old catalogues from mail order companies or department stores. Ask the children to look for, and cut out, pictures of appliances which need to be switched on and off. The children can then glue these onto a large sheet of paper for display. You may wish to allow more able children to sort them before sticking – into battery or mains supply, for example.

## Activity 7

Talk to the children about correct behaviour while using the computer (or any equipment) for safety reasons and because of the cost of the equipment. Ask the children to suggest things which they think are right and things which they think are wrong.

The photocopiable sheet provided on page 11 gives four examples of things which should not be done. These can be cut out and displayed near the computer. You can draw others to add to the display as the children suggest them (or are found doing them!). Some children might attempt to draw their own pictures and you can write underneath what they want to say.

# General Technological Awareness

### Activity 8

Show the children the mouse and demonstrate how to move it on the mouse mat. Show the cursor on the screen and how it moves. Demonstrate what happens when you lift the mouse – the cursor on screen does not move. You may wish to change the mouse settings on your computer so that it shows a trail as it moves, or so that it moves more slowly, or you could make the cursor larger.

Demonstrate the use of the left mouse button, by holding it down to move something or clicking to make something happen. This is best done using an art program, so that marks can be made on screen.

### Activity 9

Open your paint or graphics program. Select a large brush size and a colour. Allow the children free play using the mouse to make marks on the screen. Some children may be able to change colours themselves, by clicking on a different colour on the palette.

## •• Software and Hardware to support G.T.A.

Allow the children to use all kinds of programs, to help them develop their mouse skills. For example, when listening to talking stories, the children can click to change the page. Some CD-ROMs and early years' programs have activities specifically aimed at developing fine motor control.

Alternatively, there are graphics tablets now cheaply available. A graphics tablet is a flat 'slate' over which a stylus is moved, in a similar way to using a pencil on paper. Using one of these means that children having problems with pencil control or with spatial awareness difficulties need not be introduced to a different skill.

In the General Technological Awareness section of Co-ordinator's Manual 1 (Ages 4-7) details are provided of other pointing devices, such as a roller ball. This allows the child to use both hands to move the cursor while the device stays fixed on the table, thereby giving the child better control.

## •• Vocabulary

Computer, mouse, keyboard, printer, on, off

# On and Off

Computer

Calculator

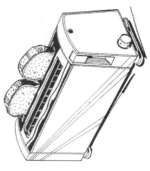

Toaster

Iron

Lamp

Electric Fan

Light Switch

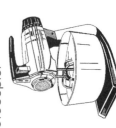

Torch

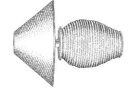

Vacuum Cleaner

Video Recorder

Photocopier

Food Mixer

TV

Personal Stereo

Fax

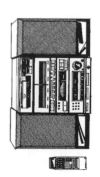

Stereo System

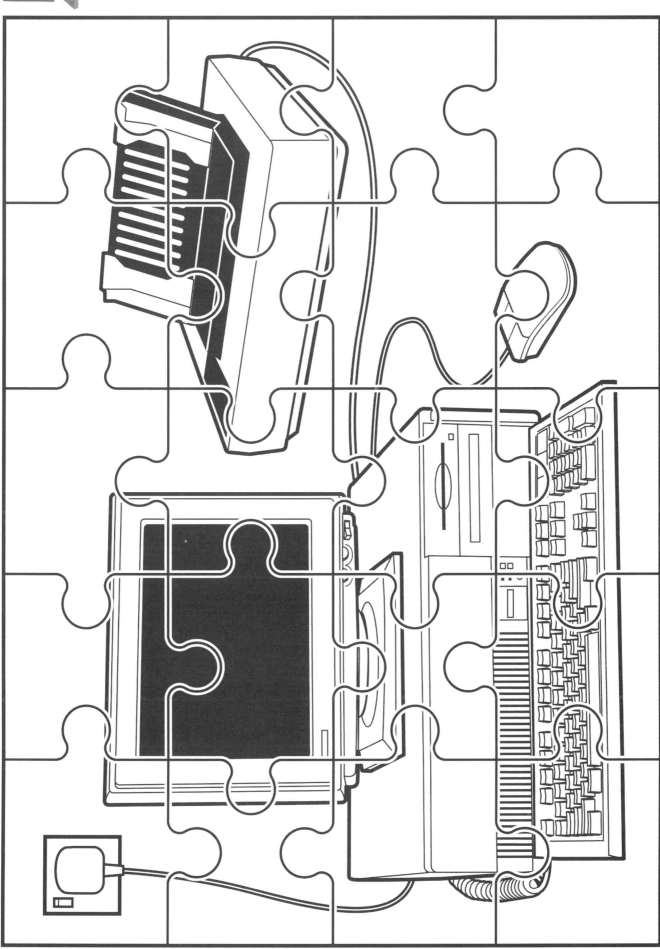

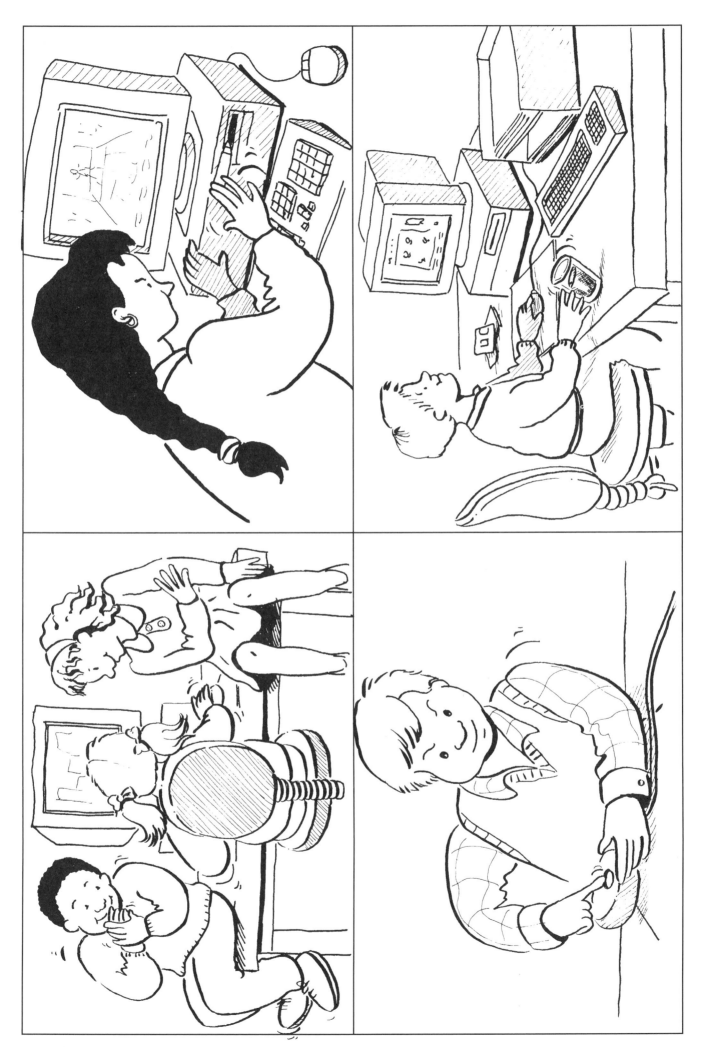

# Paint, Draw and Graphics

## •• Learning Objectives

The child can:
– experiment with mouse control
– experiment with colours
– experiment with tools.

## •• Materials

Computer with software
Printer (colour, if possible)
Mouse, tracker ball or other pointing device

## •• Teacher Information

Using a paint program is one of the most exciting ways of introducing children to the computer at an early age. The children will want to experiment with movement and colour on the screen, just as they experiment with other materials in the classroom. One advantage, of course, is that the paint program has an eraser and so clean screens can be obtained easily at any time. The children can experiment with different effects – colours and brush thickness – without worrying about spoiling the picture.

The activities are tasks for the individual at the computer and so will be quite time-consuming. Be prepared for this, but allow each child plenty of time for experimenting. The activities also provide a good way to begin practice in mouse control, however, other pointing devices are available which might be more suitable for those children who are struggling with holding a pencil (thereby ensuring that the same skills are used).

You will need to be familiar with the paint program to be used – how to change brush sizes, colours, patterns and how to save and print the children's work. For more information, see the Paint, Draw and Graphics section, Co-ordinator's Manual 1 (Ages 4–7).

## •• Activities and Teaching Points

### Activity 1

Begin by demonstrating how to move the brush around the screen, using the mouse. Some programs require the left mouse button to be held down but many early years' programs simply require a click to 'switch the brush on' and another click to switch it off again. Select the brush and a colour before the children begin and let each child experiment with making marks.

### Activity 2

Demonstrate to a small group how to change a colour by clicking on the colour palette. Again, allow each child time to experiment with making marks, lines and curves using different colours. You might want to print some of these. As printing often takes a long time (depending on the type of printer), save each file as each child finishes and choose some for printing after the session.

### Activity 3

Demonstrate to a small group how to change the thickness of the brush and allow each child to experiment. You could give them instructions for what must be included in their picture – a thick green line, a wavy blue line, a red curve, etc. You can draw these first on card and display them by the computer.

### Activity 4

Demonstrate to a small group how to use the rubber (eraser). Ask each child to draw his or her own face, using the rubber to change things if a mistake is made. Remember to save and print.

### Activity 5

Give the children a choice of things to draw, using the brush and different colours. The choice could include their pet, a house, a favourite toy, a car, their friend, etc. Remember to save and print.

### Activity 6

Show the children a different tool such as the spray can. Let each child make patterns using the spray can with different colours. Remember to save and print.

### Activity 7

Switching on the symmetry facility of your paint program while the children are experimenting with patterns will produce some exciting results. Allow each child to have several attempts until they find one which he or she likes best. Save and print the patterns.

## •• Vocabulary

Mouse, computer screen, print, paintbrush

# Word Processing

## •• Learning Objectives

The child can:
- recognise lower case letters
- match initial letters to pictures
- match simple words to pictures
- use an overlay keyboard to select lower case letters
- recognise upper case letters
- use an overlay keyboard with upper case and lower case
- understand the relative positions of keys on the keyboard
- use the return/enter key and the space bar.

## •• Materials

Computer, overlay keyboard, overlay keyboard software
Word processing progam
Sample overlays (pages 18–26)
Printer

## •• Teacher Information

Teachers need to be familiar with using a simple word processing program and using an overlay keyboard. The use of overlay keyboards is explained in detail in Co-ordinator's Manual 1 (Ages 4–7). This section explains how to set up a keyboard, and how to design and use overlays with it.

This Word Processing section should be used alongside the Keyboarding section of *I.T. Works* and should match your normal letter and word recognition activities. Young children are not able to use word processing until they have acquired recognition of some letters. The overlay keyboard provides a facility to help children towards this recognition as it can be programmed specifically to match children's development. It is important to match the I.C.T. activities closely to other activities in the classroom. The overlays provided on pages 18–24 are examples of initial letter sounds, word/picture matching, word recognition and sequencing activities.

As children begin to recognise letters, they can be introduced to the lower case letter keyboard (page 25). Children who are more able can then use the combined upper and lower case overlay (page 26). In this way, the children need not be introduced to the conventional upper case keyboard before they are ready, but can still develop communication skills through word processing. This section uses overlays with the letters in alphabetical order, but similar overlays, set out in QWERTY order, can also be designed for the more able.

All the overlay examples include options for programming keys, to enable the children to print their work, delete any mistakes, move to a new line and to make a space. In this way, the children begin to use important aspects of word processing. However, you may wish to programme cells to automatically include a space or return when pressed.

# Word Processing

## •• Activities and Teaching Points

### Activity 1

Three examples are provided for reinforcement of initial letter sounds – b, d and s. The overlay has pictures for words which begin with these letters, and some which do not. Initial work is needed on each letter sound before the children are introduced to the I.C.T. activity. You will need to programme the cells to send the words which match the pictures to the screen. Some overlay programs allow pictures as well as words to appear on screen, which would help to reinforce the correct answer, if the child does not recognise the whole word.

Introduce the activity to a group of children and demonstrate what happens when a picture is pressed. Talk about the initial letter sound and the pictures. Look at the shape of the word on the screen. Allow the children to work individually or in pairs, to complete the overlay.

More able children can be introduced to the delete, space and enter facilities and can be encouraged to print their own work. Otherwise, the space and return facilities need to be included in the cell commands after the word appears.

The overlays can also be used as an assessment activity – does the child press all the pictures or only those starting with the initial letter identified? You may wish to follow up this activity with overlays of your own for other initial letter sounds and then for letter blends.

### Activity 2

The overlay, 'Matching' (see page 21), continues the activities on initial letter sounds but this time the child is asked to recognise the picture and the word. Introduce this activity when doing other picture/word matching activities in the classroom.

You will need to programme the cells under the words and the cells under the pictures so that they send the same word to the screen. You may need to programme the word cells to include a space after the word, and the picture cells to include a return, so that each one is on a new line. More able children should be encouraged to use the space bar and return/enter key on the overlay.

Demonstrate what happens when a word is pressed. Look at the shape of the word on the screen. Ask the child to press the picture which matches that word. The same word appears next to the first one – so the child can check whether or not he or she is correct.

### Activity 3

The overlay, 'Body Matching' (see page 22), is an example of a word/picture matching activity which is designed to support topic work in Nursery, Reception and P1. Demonstrate to a group of children how to press a word, then press its matching picture. The same word should appear twice on screen, so that the children know whether they are right or wrong.

# Word Processing

## Activity 4

The overlay, 'All About Me' (see page 23), introduces the children to completing simple sentences without the difficulty of finding all the individual letters on the keyboard. This is their introduction to word processing.

The children using this overlay need to be able to recognise numbers and the letters of their name. Full stop and shift keys are included on the overlay. These should be used only if children ask for them. Some children may want to start their name with a capital letter. The activity is best introduced to a small group of children, with one child pressing the cells to show what happens. Demonstrate how to print their work. Some children may wish to print two copies so that one can be taken home.

## Activity 5

The overlay, 'Little Miss Muffet' (see page 24), is designed to support sequencing activities already taking place in the classroom. The children have to press the pictures in the correct order of the nursery rhyme. Text (and pictures, if your program allows it) will appear on the screen.

This activity is best carried out as a small group activity working with an adult. The children can say the line from the nursery rhyme as the picture is pressed. The version on screen can then be read back to the children, to check whether it is in the correct order. The adult can then show how easy it is to correct mistakes, by deleting a wrong line and pressing the correct picture. The text can be printed out for each child, so that they can draw a picture.

## Activity 6

Two overlays are provided – one containing lower case letters in alphabetical order and one with both lower and upper case letters, again in alphabetical order (see pages 25–26). These are provided because alphabet work in the classroom teaches children to identify a letter in its place in alphabetical order. To introduce another order of letters (i.e. the QWERTY order of the computer keyboard) would be confusing at this stage.

These overlays can be used by children in the emergent writing stage who wish to use I.C.T. to write words or short sentences. Some sentence beginnings and key words written on card can be displayed near the computer for the children to use.
For example,
I like
My friend is
I have
etc.
Demonstrate how to use the overlays to small groups before allowing the children to experiment with them. The return/enter key, space bar and delete keys will need explaining.

Be careful when planning word processing prwork, as children's I.C.T. skills may not match their writing skills.

# Word Processing

### Overlay Ideas

Overlays can be made for the following purposes:
- to reinforce your reading scheme, with pictures of the characters, their names, key words, etc.
- to sequence stories such as 'The Three Little Pigs'
- to sequence the children's journey to school
- to sequence the school day

(The above sequencing activities can be carried out with a group drawing their own pictures first which can be used to make the overlays. The children can narrate the stories in their own words for the teacher to type into the computer, so that the children's own words appear on screen).
- to produce picture/word matching activities of items in the home or classroom
- to carry out short sentence work, using words or pictures on the overlay about today's weather
- to produce word banks for topics.

There are endless possibilities. Modern overlay keyboards for multimedia computers allow sounds or speech to be heard when cells are pressed. This adds another dimension – allowing the teacher to record key words from the reading scheme, or sentences to be heard when writing appears on-screen.

## •• Vocabulary

Keyboard, space bar, enter, delete, print

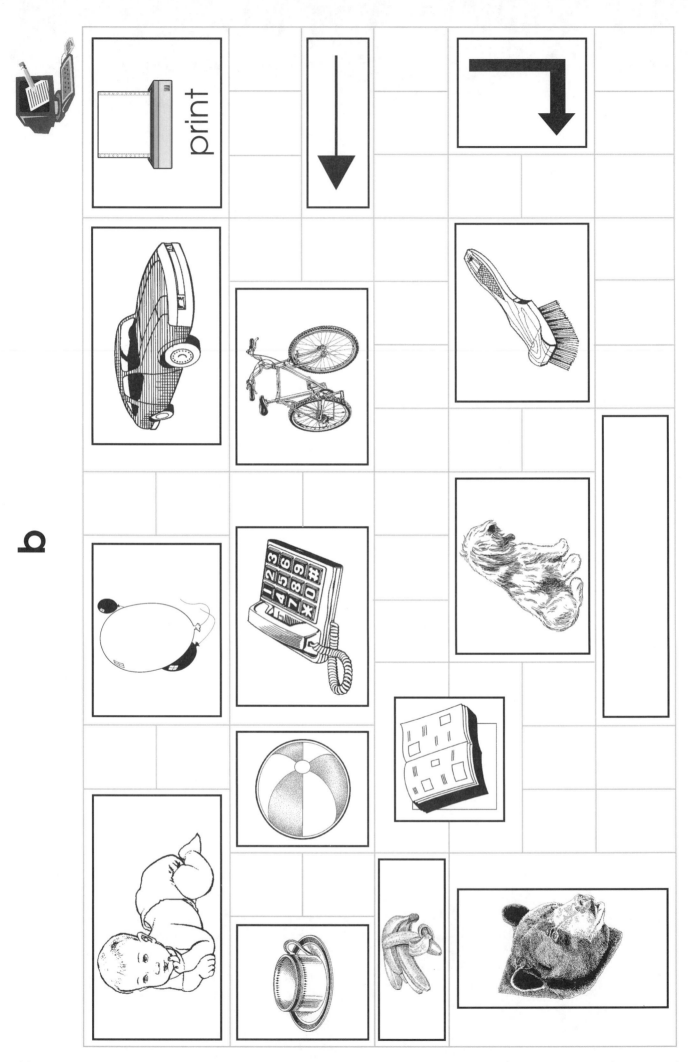

print

18

© Folens (copiable page)

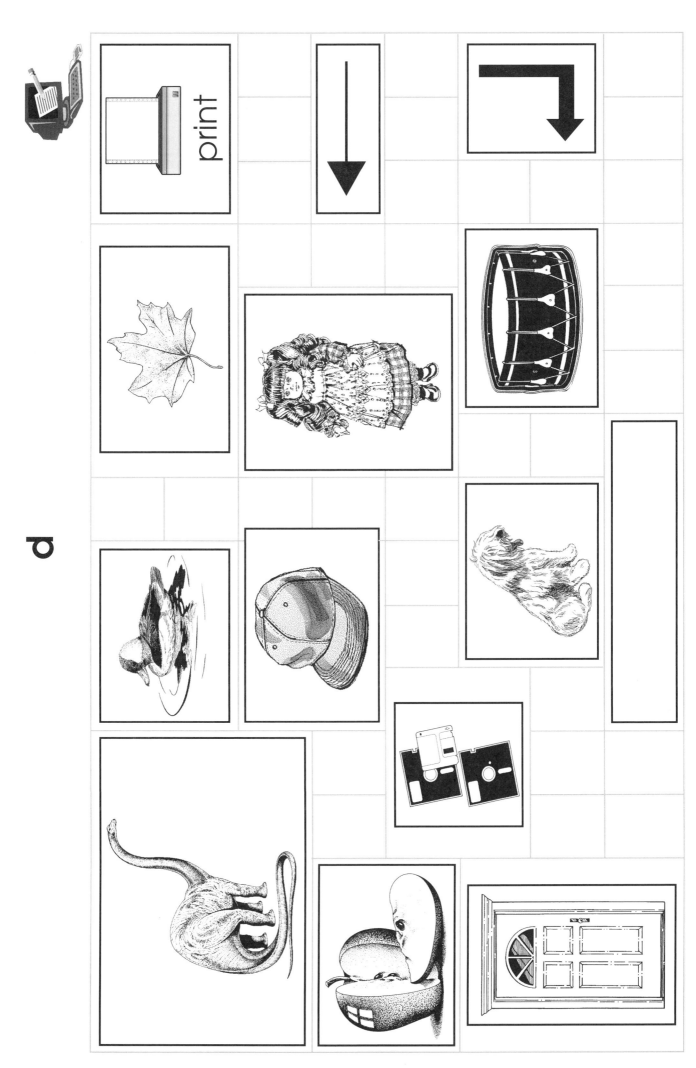

**d**

print

s

print

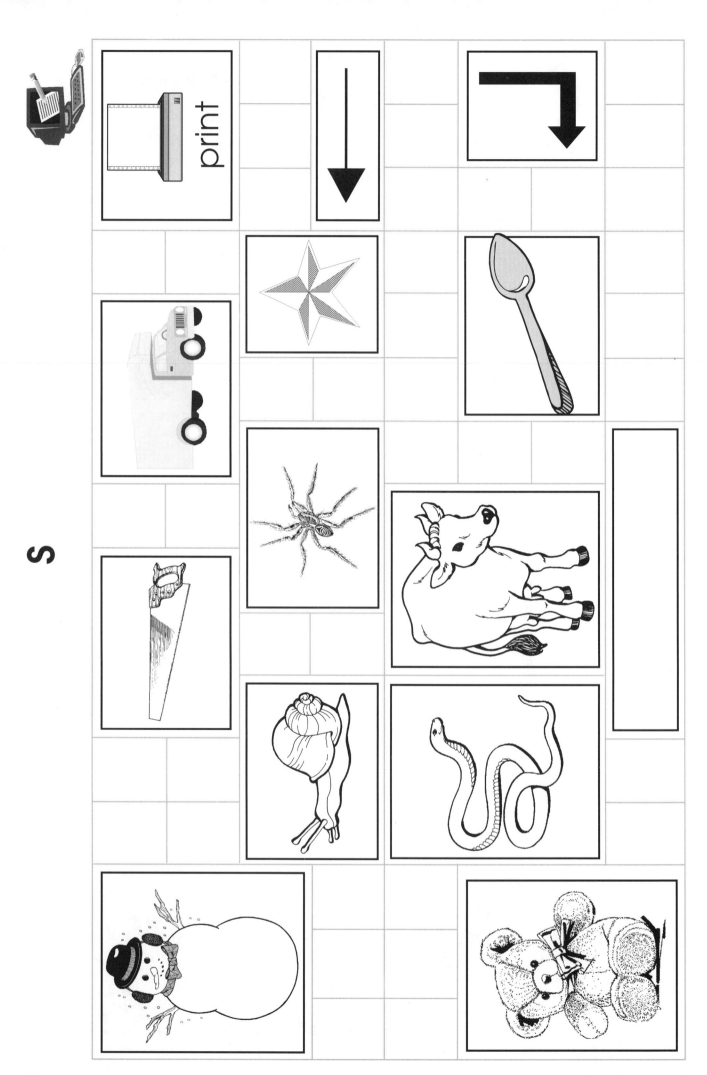

# Matching

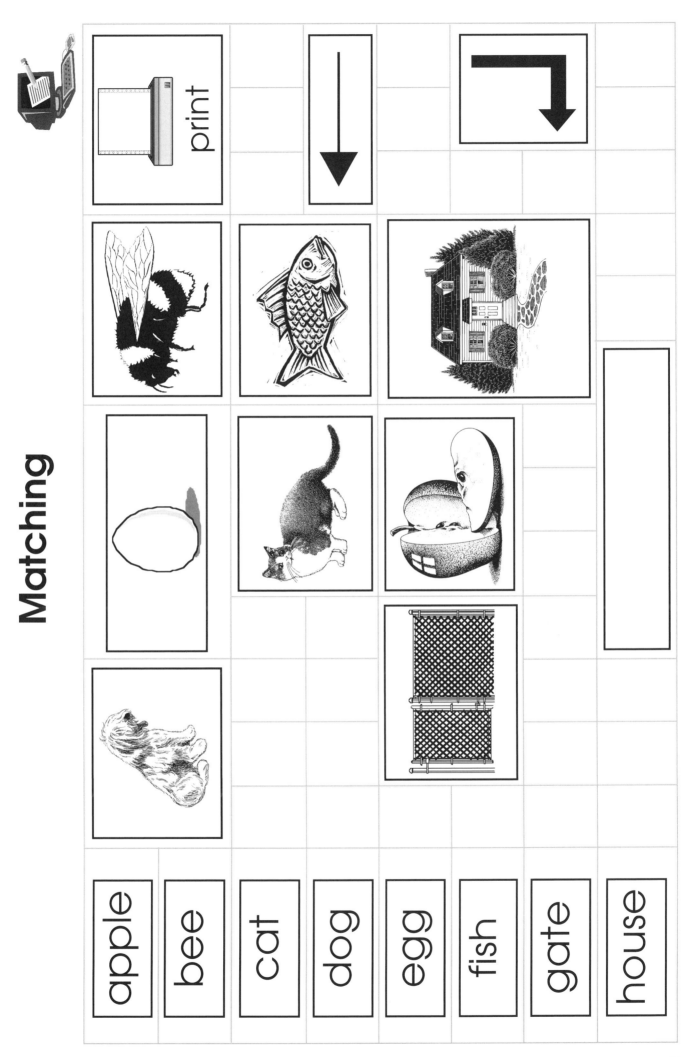

print

apple

bee

cat

dog

egg

fish

gate

house

# Body Matching

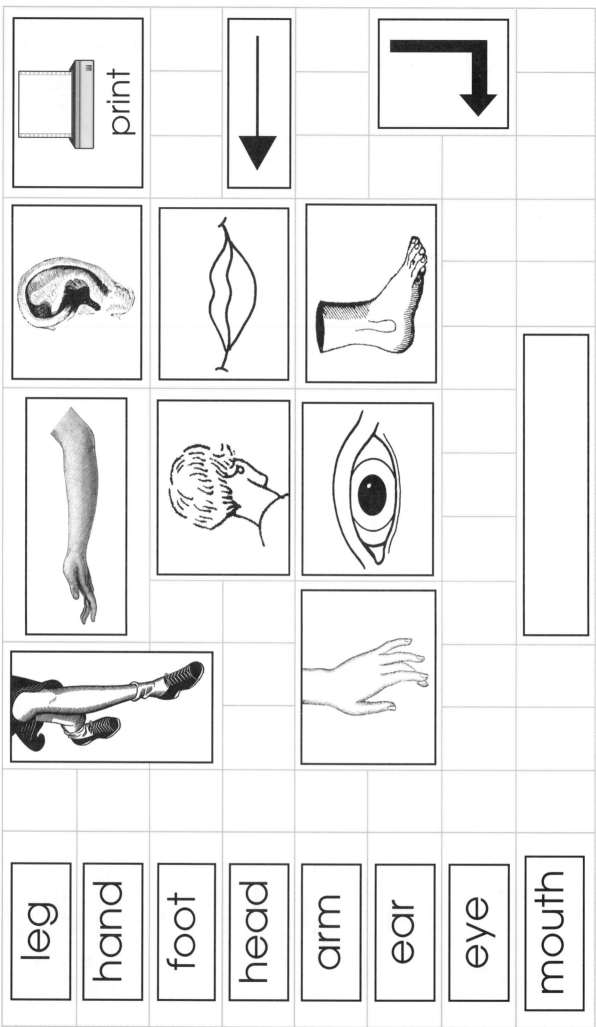

print

leg

hand

foot

head

arm

ear

eye

mouth

# All About Me

print

sisters

girl

and

| | | | | | . |
|---|---|---|---|---|---|

My name is

I am a

boy

I am

years old

I have

brothers

| 0 | 1 | 2 | 3 | 4 | 5 | 6 | 7 | 8 | 9 |
|---|---|---|---|---|---|---|---|---|---|

| a | b | c | d | e | f | g | h | i | j | k | l | m |
|---|---|---|---|---|---|---|---|---|---|---|---|---|
| n | o | p | q | r | s | t | u | v | w | x | y | z |

# Little Miss Muffet

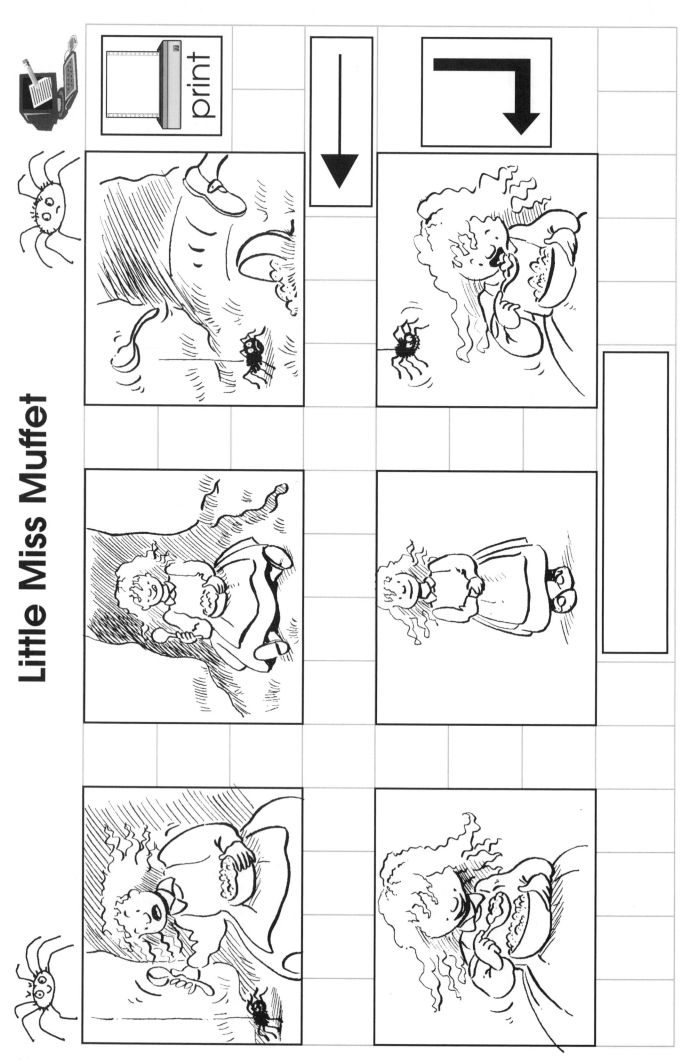

# Alphabetical Order

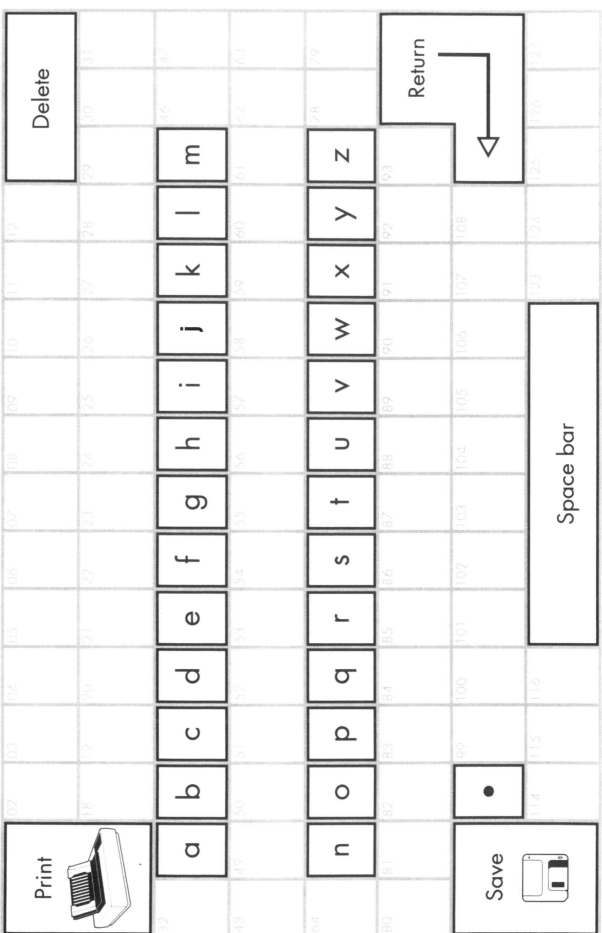

Delete

Return

Space bar

a b c d e f g h i j k l m

n o p q r s t u v w x y z

Print

Save

# Upper and Lower Case

| Delete | | Print | Return | | | |
|---|---|---|---|---|---|---|
| | m | z | | M | Z | Save |
| | l | y | | L | Y | |
| | k | x | | K | X | Space bar |
| | j | w | | J | W | |
| | i | v | | I | V | |
| | h | u | | H | U | |
| | g | t | | G | T | |
| | f | s | | F | S | |
| | e | r | | E | R | |
| | d | q | | D | Q | • |
| | c | p | | C | P | |
| | b | o | | B | O | |
| | a | n | | A | N | |

# Keyboarding

## •• Learning Objectives

The child can:
- recognise lower case letters
- match initial letters to pictures
- match simple words to pictures
- use an overlay keyboard to select lower case letters
- recognise upper case letters
- use an overlay keyboard with upper case and lower case
- identify the space bar, return/enter key and delete/backspace key.

## •• Materials

Computer
Word processing program
Paper keyboards (on pages 30–31)
Large cut-outs of keys (teacher-made)
Overlay keyboard and overlay design software
Upper and lower case QWERTY keyboard overlay (see page 32)

## •• Teacher Information

This section should be completed after the Word Processing section and should match your normal letter and word recognition activities. Young children are not able to use the keyboard until they have acquired recognition of upper and lower case letters, so care should be taken before moving children on. Teaching keyboarding skills at this early age will consist of familiarising the children with the relative positions of letter keys through games and play activities. More able children can be introduced to the space bar, return/enter key and the delete key as they move on to using the actual keyboard. The Keyboarding sections in later Units introduce children to the correct placement of fingers as their hands grow and can reach the appropriate keys.

## •• Activities and Teaching Points

These activities are best done with a small group and an adult. They can be carried out with photocopied paper keyboards so that the children can colour them, or you may wish to laminate a set of paper keyboards for the children to use with washable marker pens.

### Activity 1

Give each child a copy of the lower case paper keyboard. Ask the children to colour in the letters of their name.

### Activity 2

Give each child a copy of the lower case keyboard. Play 'keyboard bingo'. Ask each child to colour any five letters on their keyboard (you can vary the number of letters depending on the children). Call out letters, placing large letter cards where the children can see them. The children should cover their coloured letter if it is called out. You may wish to make a set of laminated, coloured bingo keyboards which can be used again.

# Keyboarding

A word card can be given to each child at the beginning as an alternative to selecting their own letters to colour. The children start by colouring in the letters on the keyboard to match the word given.

## Activity 3

Make a set of large cut-out letters (you can put lower and upper case on each card) and laminate them. Place the letter cards in the correct QWERTY order. Give each child in the group a letter to find and hold up. You can hold up word cards so that more able children find a group of letters.

## Activity 4

Place the large cut-out letter cards on the floor, in the correct QWERTY order, but well spread out. Play a game where the children put their hands and feet on letters which are called out and so become all twisted up. For example, put your first foot on the letter S, a hand on the letter P, etc.

## Activity 5

Make large word cards of key words, topic words or characters from your reading scheme. Ask each child to pick a word card, they must then pick up the large cut-out letters to cover the matching letters on the word card.

## Activity 6

Give the children pictures with different initial letter sounds and a paper keyboard. Ask the children to colour the initial letter on the keyboard. This activity can be repeated using the full word for the more able children.

## Activity 7

Photocopy an upper case keyboard and stick it onto card. Laminate it, then cut out the individual letters. Give a paper lower case keyboard to a group of children and ask them to cover each lower case letter with its matching upper case letter. This will probably need to be done with small groups of letters to begin with, and will need to be repeated several times.

## Activity 8

Photocopy a lower case keyboard and stick it onto card. Laminate it, then cut out the individual letters. These letters can now be mixed with the upper case letters. Share the letters out with a small group and play the game of snap. The children should match a lower case with an upper case letter to say "snap". Anyone can call "snap" at any time.

## Activity 9

Some of the activities above, such as keyboard bingo, can be repeated but using the upper case paper keyboards. Children need to be confident in recognising both upper and lower case letters before moving on to the conventional keyboard. At this early age, only a small group might be ready to move on to this activity.

# Keyboarding

### Activity 10

Make an overlay file for the overlay 'Upper and Lower Case Keyboard' (page 32). Provide each child with a word card to copy using the overlay keyboard. This consolidates the recognition of upper and lower case letters. This activity can be repeated with other similar ones before the children move on to using the conventional keyboard. For example, the children can supply words or a sentence for an adult to write for them. The children can then copy these words or sentences, using the overlay keyboard.

### Activity 11

Ask the children to make labels for the classroom using the upper and lower case overlay, e.g. door, window, desk, etc. This links keyboarding skills to word processing.

### Activity 12

Use the upper and lower case overlay keyboard to demonstrate the delete key, space bar and return/enter keys. Ask the children to tell you their news for you to write down – perhaps two sentences underneath each other. The children can use the overlay to copy and print their sentences.

Following these activities, some children may be able to continue word processing using the conventional keyboard for emergent writing. Display a large upper and lower case keyboard near the computer, for reference.

## •• Vocabulary

Keyboard, capital letter, space bar, delete, enter

# Lower Case Keyboard

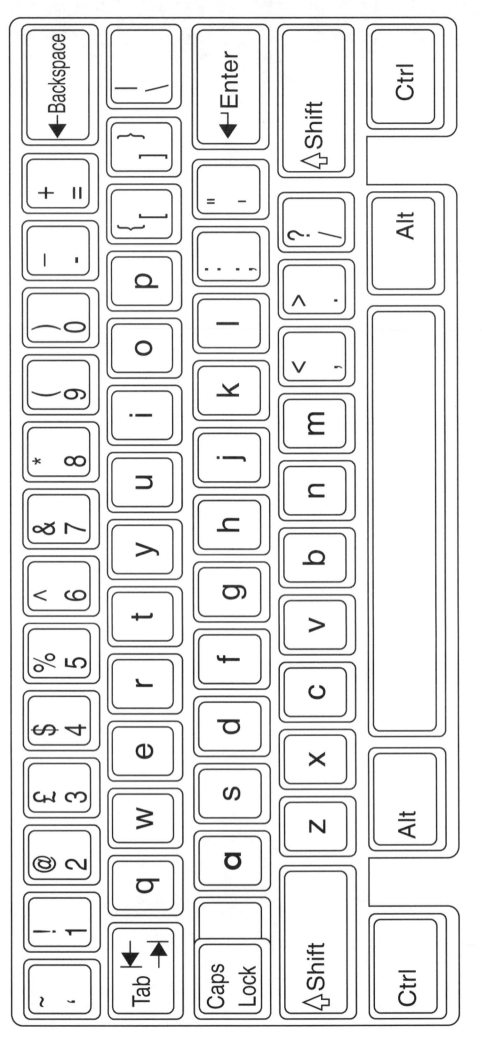

# Upper Case Keyboard

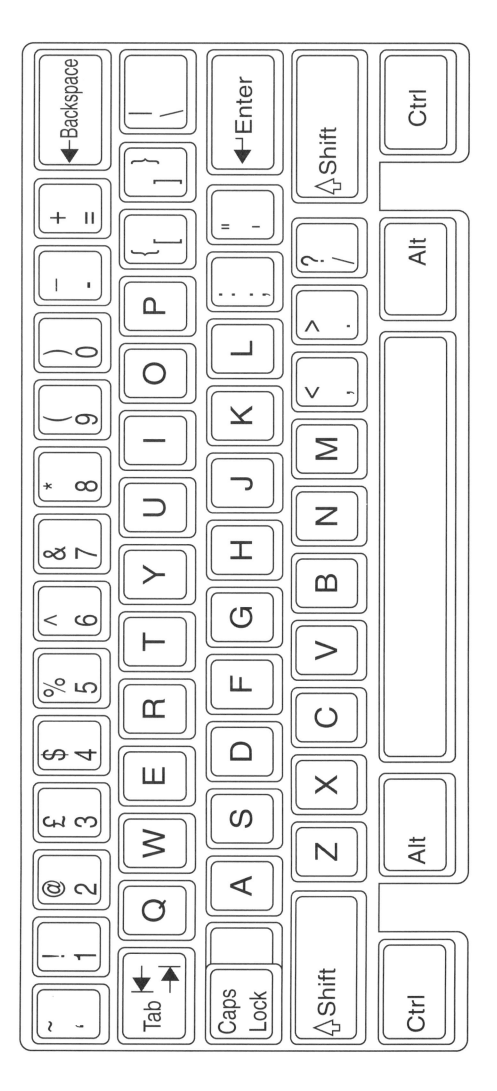

# Upper and Lower Case Keyboard

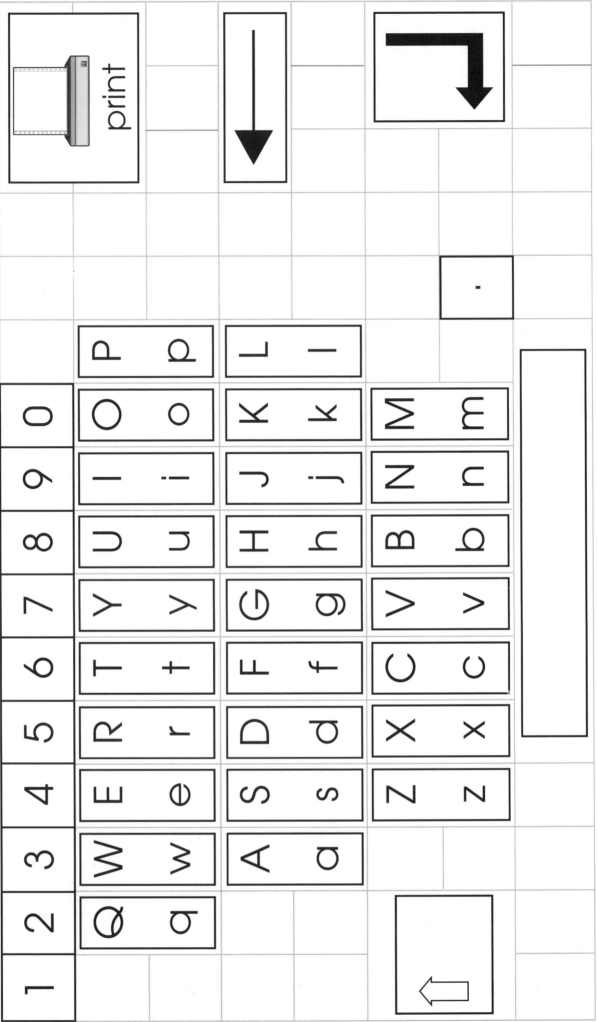

| 1 | 2 | 3 | 4 | 5 | 6 | 7 | 8 | 9 | 0 |
|---|---|---|---|---|---|---|---|---|---|
| Q | W | E | R | T | Y | U | I | O | P |
| q | w | e | r | t | y | u | i | o | p |
| A | S | D | F | G | H | J | K | L | |
| a | s | d | f | g | h | j | k | l | |
| Z | X | C | V | B | N | M | | | |
| z | x | c | v | b | n | m | | | |

print

# Control

## •• Learning Objectives

The child can:
- understand that control is an important aspect in everyday life
- control devices purposefully by turning devices on and off
- sequence instructions in order
- understand forward and backward
- understand left and right
- experiment with turns
- give separate commands to a partner to move
- give a series of commands to a partner
- enter the forward command into a programmable toy (Roamer)
- clear a command
- use the forward, CM and GO commands
- use the backward command
- enter the right and left turn commands.

## •• Materials

Roamer or other programmable toy
Appliances (or toys) which will turn on and off
Photocopiable sheets (pages 39–45)

## •• Teacher Information

There are many instances in real life where the children will experience computer control of everyday items. These experiences can form a starting point for early years' role-play and activities preparing for an understanding of computer control. A good place to begin is by looking at appliances which you already have in the classroom and then to move on to 'control' of a toy, such as a Roamer or Pixie. You need to be familiar with how a Roamer works, and how to programme the units of movement and turn. The activities at this age assume that the Roamer is programmed to turns of a right angle. You may also wish to change the units of forward and backward to smaller units, depending on the amount of space in your room (units are pre-set to 1 length of the Roamer).

An essential task when using a Roamer is to ensure that children become used to pressing CM before entering new commands. This clears the memory and is an important command for the children to learn. For more information, see the Control Section of Co-ordinator's Manual 1 (Ages 4-7).

There is a wide choice of activities suggested in this section, many of which are group activities. Choose the activities which are most appropriate for your children and the space available.

# Control

## •• Activities and Teaching Points

### Activity 1 (on-going)

Role-play is an essential part of the early years' curriculum, so when planning your role-play areas for the year, try to include some aspects of control. Here are some ideas which help to develop children's awareness of control elements in everyday life:

- Home corner – include a cooker, washing machine, fridge, microwave, dishwasher. These can be items of normal home corner equipment or items made by the children.
- A supermarket – include a checkout with a barcode scanner, a till, conveyor belt for goods, an automatic door, food freezers.
- An airport – include a ticket office, a currency exchange, passport control, luggage check, the inside of an aircraft.
- A café – include a cooker, dishwasher, fridge, freezer, cash tills.
- A garage – include petrol pumps, tills, a carwash, an air pump.
- A factory – include machines which make goods, conveyor belts, fork lift trucks, computers, packing machines.
- A Bank, Building Society or Post Office – include cash tills, computers, automatic doors, alarm systems, wall money machines.

In any role-play area, spend some time with groups of children talking about what they are doing and discussing the control elements, by asking questions such as –
"Which things are done by hand and which by machines?"
"What does this machine/item/appliance do?"
"Who operates this machine/item/appliance?"
"How does this machine/item/appliance work?"
"What do people come here for?"

Try to follow up at least one role-play area idea with a visit. A visit to a supermarket, for instance, can include experience and recognition of many areas of control as well as supporting other areas of the curriculum.

### Activity 2

The photocopiable pictures 'At the Garage' (see page 39), 'In the Kitchen' (see page 40), 'In the Supermarket' (see page 41), show examples of control in everyday life. Work with a small group of children to identify where the control elements are. Talk about which machines are started by people but then do other things automatically. Discuss what people have to do and what is done automatically by the machine. Encourage the children to think about how the machines can work automatically.

The three examples provided are places which the children are likely to know. They can discuss differences between the pictures and their own experiences. After the discussion, ask the children to mark, circle, or colour the devices which are controlled.

# Control

## Activity 3

Provide catalogues, brochures or magazines for children to identify examples of control and then cut them out. Some children might be able to sort these into things which can be found in the kitchen, living room, garage, etc. These can be stuck onto large pieces of paper for display.

## Activity 4

An important part of later control work is the ability to sequence instructions, to make the computer or programmable toy do something. Being able to break down a problem into manageable parts is an important skill. With a small group of children, play games in which you first give them a single command to carry out then gradually build up to a sequence of instructions (depending on the ability of the children). Games such as 'Simon Says' are an excellent example.

Ask the children to talk about everyday activities and the order in which they do them, for example what exactly do they do when they go to wash their hands? Can they include all the details in the correct order?

## Activity 5

Use the photocopiable sheet 'Getting Ready for School' (see page 42). This is an example of a picture sequencing activity where the children are given a situation – "What do we need to do to get ready for school?" – and they need to think about the separate activities which need to be done. The children, of course, may want to add more pictures of their own. Ask the children to colour the pictures, then cut them out and glue them in the correct order. This can be followed up with many other similar sequencing activities. For example,
- the order of the school day
- a set of instructions for making toast
- a set of instructions for getting ready for home time.

## Activity 6

Next, the children can begin to give instructions to each other. Initially, these instructions should be to carry out a certain job in the classroom, e.g. pick up the toys; pick up the toys and put them in the box; pick up the toys, put them in the box and put the box in the cupboard, etc. Ask children to take 'control' at tidy up time with a partner, one giving instructions to another to clear something away.

The children can sit in a circle and play games where instructions are given to the person next to them.

# Control

## Activity 7

Once the children are confident with giving 'commands' or instructions, you can introduce specific movement commands in preparation for controlling the programmable toy. Commands such as forward, backward, turn left and turn right can be introduced in the classroom and in P.E. activities. Children can work in pairs to direct each other to a certain part of the room, around one or more objects, or to the teacher. You will need to discuss how to move forward – does the partner move forward until he or she hits the obstacle, or by a certain number of steps? How much does the partner turn? At this point, it is a good idea to introduce a quarter turn as the unit of turn. Make sure that the children understand the word 'turn' and that they should stay on the spot while they turn.

The photocopiable sheet 'Left and Right' (see page 43) can be cut and mounted on card so that children can hold each symbol in the correct hand. The person giving commands can hold the symbol cards to help them with directions and the 'robot' can hold the cards to help them follow the commands.

## Activity 8

Take photographs of people at work in different areas around school, e.g. the secretary in the office, the headteacher in the school hall, the cook in the kitchen, etc. Mount the photographs and laminate. Working with a small group of children, give each child a photograph and, starting at the classroom door, give directions for one child acting as a 'robot' to go to the area in the first photograph. Let each child have a turn at being the robot. Commands are given in forward or backward paces and quarter turns. The left and right symbol cards can also be used to help.

## Activity 9

Use P.E. apparatus in the hall to build simple obstacle courses. The children may work in groups to do this, making an obstacle course for another group to use. Children must then give directions to a 'robot' to move around their course.

## Activity 10

When the children have practised giving commands to each other, a Roamer or programmable toy can be introduced. Begin by sitting a group of children in a circle and allowing each of them to enter FORWARD and a number into the Roamer, to send it to someone else in the circle. The person who receives the Roamer picks it up, turns it to point to someone else and sends it to them.

You will need to show the children how to press CM before they enter their command (describe this as rubbing out the last person's command).

## Activity 11

Repeat the circle activity but when a child receives the Roamer, they must use the BACKWARD command to send the Roamer back to the sender, without picking it up. The sender can programme the Roamer to go to someone else in the circle.

## Activity 12

Build a stack of plastic or light building blocks. Place the Roamer a distance away and ask the children to programme the Roamer to move forward and knock over as many blocks as possible.

## Activity 13

Make a number line on the floor, using large card numbers or carpet squares. Each child should put the Roamer at the start and send the Roamer forward to land on the number of their age. They might need to try this a few times.

## Activity 14

Introduce LEFT and RIGHT to a small group and allow them to take the Roamer on a walk around the classroom. Begin by planning a route yourself and making cards for the commands which would send the Roamer around your route. A photocopiable sheet of commands is provided on page 44 so that you can make laminated cards – numbers can be added with washable marker pens. In this way, the children can begin by copying your commands into the Roamer. (Remember to programme the right and left turns to 90°).

## Activity 15

Repeat the above activity as a treasure trail. Make a different trail but at certain points the children have to collect something, such as toy people or animals. The collection points can be marked on the cards or separate cards can be inserted into the list of commands. The children could devise a way of making a box or carrier for the Roamer to carry the objects they have collected.

## Activity 16

A simple obstacle course can be set as a challenge for the more able children. This can be built using construction apparatus or building blocks – perhaps in the hall or corridor. Ask a small group to see if they can send the Roamer around the course. An adult can scribe their commands. You can then discuss with the children what they have done. More able children may be able to suggest changes – such as making Forward 2 CM Forward 2 into Forward 4.

## Activity 17

Use a floor map, or build a simple 3D map from boxes. Children can make their own houses or shops to form an imaginary village. The Roamer can be dressed up as a postal worker and the children can programme it to visit different houses.

## Activity 18

The photocopiable sheet, 'Going To School', on page 45 provides a game to reinforce the commands. The sheet can be photocopied, coloured, stuck on card and laminated, or the children could be given copies to colour in themselves. You will need to make a spinner which has commands and symbols on it. This works best with a nail through the centre, fixed to a piece of wood so that it spins easily. Children can play in pairs or threes, placing a toy car or figure on a starting arrow, then taking turns to move one square at a time to see who can get to school first. When the spinner chooses a left or right turn, the player must turn their object without moving to a different square. If a forward or backward move is chosen but the player's object is facing a building, they must miss their turn. You may wish to enlarge the sheet to A3 before using.

3D buildings can also be made from small boxes and decorated by the children, then placed on the sheet.

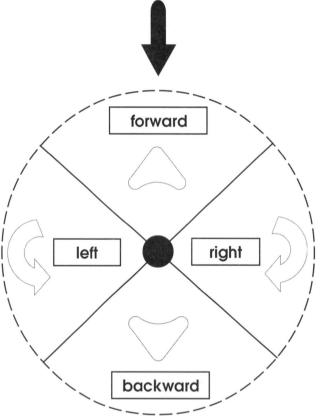

## •• Vocabulary

Commands, left, right, forward, backward, clear memory

# At the Garage

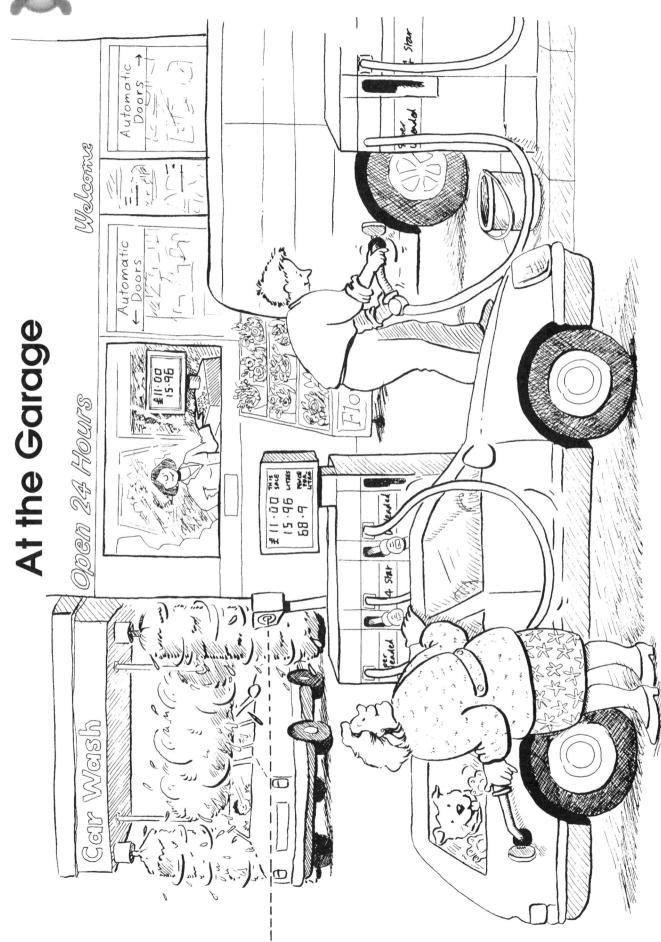

# In the Kitchen

# In the Supermarket

# Getting Ready For School

# Left and Right

right

left

# Roamer Commands

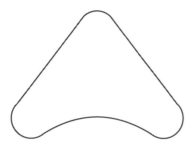

forward

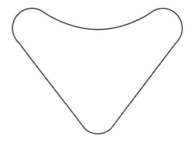

backward

clear memory

go

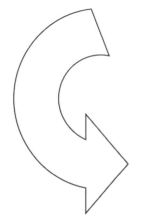

turn left

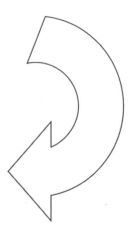

turn right

# Going To School

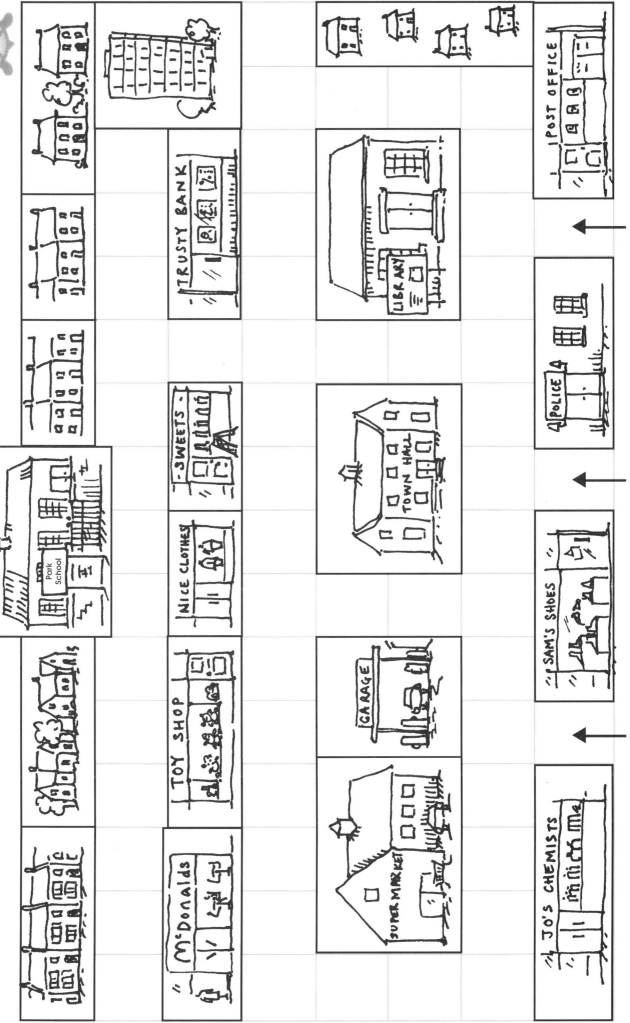

# Video

## •• Learning Objectives

The child can:
- use role-play to develop speaking skills
- use role-play to develop social/co-operative skills
- experiment with the use of a camcorder in the classroom
- speak clearly to a camera
- maintain eye contact with the camera
- understand the functions of a camcorder
- locate the controls on a camcorder
- switch the camera on and off
- start and stop recording.

## •• Materials

Camcorder with tapes
Tripod
Small TV to use as a monitor (optional)

## •• Teacher Information

Using a video (or camcorder) in Nursery/Reception/P1 is an excellent way to develop children's communication skills, self-control and independence. When making video films, the children will also need to work as part of a group, so social skills will also be developed (taking turns, waiting for others, sharing, etc). Use of a camcorder can enhance activities, such as role-play, which already take place in the classroom. Children today will all have had plenty of experience of TV and will accept the activity just as any other.

It is important, at first, to make sure that the camera is firmly fixed on a tripod. Do not let the children carry it freely around the classroom because of all the other activities taking place. The tripod is best set up near a wall or fixed furniture, so that the rear two legs are on either side of the camera person. In this way, children will be deterred from trying to push round behind the camera when filming. If possible, this should also be in a place where the major light source is behind the camera. If you have a small TV, it is a good idea to connect the video out (or aerial lead) to this, so that the children in the group can see easily what is being filmed. For more information, see the Video section, Co-ordinator's Manual 1 (Ages 4–7).

# Video

## •• Activities and Teaching Points

### Activity 1

Show the children the camera and demonstrate how it works. At this stage, they will just need to use the red start and pause button (make sure that the camera is switched on to record). If you have the camera connected to a TV, demonstrate how to move the camera slowly and carefully by filming each of the children's faces. Show what happens when the camera moves too quickly – we cannot follow the picture with our eyes.

You will need to demonstrate how to look through the viewfinder. Young children often find this difficult to co-ordinate and film the ceiling without understanding why they are not seeing anything!

### Activity 2

Allow each child to record an activity in the classroom. A partner should stand next to the camera so that he or she can talk about what or who is being filmed. Later, replay the recordings and talk about what the children have seen and heard, and the sequence of the day. Be prepared for this to take some time – you may need to do some simple editing to cut the film short. (See the Video section, Co-ordinator's Manual 1, for more information). You may wish to set a time limit for each child for this activity.

### Activity 3

Allow a group to make a film of their role-play. This is the start of the children making a short film – with a beginning and an end. Talk to the children first about what sort of things they do in the role-play area, how they come into it and when they will stop. Decide together who will do the filming and who will be the actors.

### Activity 4

When the children are more confident at speaking in school, allow pairs to film each other. They can introduce themselves, speaking their name, age and what they like to do in school. You will need to show the class where to stand or sit when being filmed – how far away from the camera they should be, and how to sit or stand up straight. At this point, it is a good idea to introduce the 'thumbs up' sign as a signal to start speaking. (The tape takes a second or two to begin turning and recording sound, so starting to speak too soon misses the beginning). You could suggest that the camera person presses the red button, counts "1, 2, 3", then gives the thumbs up sign. Some children may need another helper to do this for them.

### Activity 5

As children start to read books, or look at the pictures and make up their own stories, make a 'Story Time' video. A small group or individual can sit and read or tell a story while a partner records them. Later, allow the rest of the class to sit, watch and listen. If possible, allow the children to take the tape home to show their family, or invite their parents to a video showing.

# Video

### Activity 6

As a link to early geography activities, take a small group of children to film different parts of the school grounds. The group can go out first with an adult to decide which parts they will film. Each child in the group can film a different part, with another standing close to the camera to describe what they can see there. It is a good idea to keep the camera on the tripod, to be carried by the adult to each location.

### Activity 7

Talk with the children about people who are important to us in our school – the headteacher, secretary, site supervisor, welfare staff, cleaners, cook. Arrange for groups of children to 'interview' each person. Some may be able to ask questions but the activity should be aimed at giving the children confidence with the camera. The completed films can be watched back in class and talked about with the children.

### Activity 8

If you have a link school, the class can make a video about your school to send to the other school. The children can talk first about what they would like to show other children – different classrooms, a P.E. lesson, classroom activities, playtime, etc. Confident children can record a simple introduction first. You may also wish to introduce titles here, by painting a big 'Our School' sign for the children to record.

### Activity 9

Once the children are confident in using the camera, and are confident in front of the camera, why not hold a talent show, where the children decide what they would like to do in front of the camera. Some children are more likely to perform in front of a camera with only a friend watching than in front of an audience.

## •• Vocabulary

Camera, tripod, record, tape

# Information Handling

## ·· Learning Objectives

The child can:
- understand that information can be stored
- use role-play to simulate real-life information handling
- sort objects in the classroom in an order
- classify or group a variety of objects
- classify objects according to two criteria
- search for and choose an object in response to a question
- add a picture to a class pictogram
- answer simple questions about a pictogram
- collect data
- present data using a pictogram.

## ·· Materials

Materials for sorting and classifying
Photocopiable sheets (pages 53–60)

## ·· Teacher Information

Sorting is the earliest preparation for information handling, and is a common activity in early years' classrooms. Sorting objects by different criteria (colour, shape, size, etc.) is an essential part in the child's development towards being able to critically analyse information later in school. Therefore, many Information Handling activities in Nursery, Reception and P1 do not necessarily require the use of a computer.

At an early age, children can carry out role-play, simulating places and activities where information handling is used in real life – in a bank, supermarket, post office, travel agent, etc. The activities provided concentrate on practical activities (off the computer), which support and develop information handling skills. These skills can be transferred to the computer later. The activities need to include lots of practice in sorting and classifying different objects, materials, etc.

Lots of information in early years' classrooms can be displayed as pictograms and graphs. For example, pictograms of favourite food or flower colour can be used as an early introduction to graphs. Again, it is important to ask questions about the data that is displayed, so that children can begin to interpret the data they see.

Such questions might include: "How many children like yellow flowers?" The next stage is to introduce a data handling program on the computer, which allows pictograms to be made by pressing a key or using a mouse. For more information, see the Information Handling section, Co-ordinator's Manual 1 (Ages 4-7).

# Information Handling

## •• Activities and Teaching Points

### Activity 1 (on-going)

The sorting activities which take place every day in a Nursery, Reception or P1 classroom are the foundation for being able to handle data in a variety of ways. Give the children plenty of opportunities to sort objects, pictures, appliances in the classroom according to different criteria. To link with I.C.T., you could ask children to sort appliances which are operated by hand from those which are operated by some other form of energy (an example photocopiable sheet is provided on page 53).

### Activity 2

The next stage to introduce to the children is sorting by two criteria – for example, which shapes are red and round, which are blue and round? Which are yellow squares and which are green squares? The children can sort themselves by their colour of hair, colour of eyes, what type of clothes they are wearing, etc.

### Activity 3

A photocopiable sheet 'Information About ...' is provided on page 54 which enables children to sort objects or pictures in a simple Venn diagram. Alternatively, you can use large coloured hoops on the floor. It is important that children have experience of various types of Boolean sorting methods, such as Venn diagrams, as they move through school, in preparation for searching a large database or the Internet later. At this early level, sorting using a Venn diagram is best introduced as a group activity using just two choices.

For example,

I can hop, I can skip, I can do both.

I like sausages, I like beans, I like both.

# Information Handling

## Activity 4

Role-play areas can introduce the children to understanding that information can be stored, and that it is very common in the world around us. Discuss with the children places which store information – such as banks, building societies and supermarkets. A visit with the children would be very useful. The children might be able to visit the school office, to see how information about them is stored.

Try to incorporate this aspect in your role-play areas. You may have a role-play area of a bank and could allow the children a certain amount of toy money which they can put in or take out. If you have a role-play shop, a record of how many items are on the shelves needs to be kept.

## Activity 5

A common activity in early years is to collect information about the day's weather. The photocopiable sheet 'What's The Weather Like?' (see page 55) provides symbols which you can use with the children to stick on a daily weather chart. At the end of a week, it is important to talk to the children about the record and ask them questions about the information which they have collected. The symbols will need photocopying so that you have a collection of each. They could also be coloured in by the children.

Programs are available if you wish to link this activity to the computer. For example, you could use a simple program which involves dressing a teddy in suitable clothes for the weather.

## Activity 6

You may wish to use your computer and an overlay keyboard alongside your wall chart to record the information, as a teacher-led activity. Use the overlay on page 59, 'This Week's Weather', to send the name of the day to the screen and a simple description of the weather. For example, pressing Monday then the cloud would send 'Monday is cloudy' to the screen. This can be done using a word processor at this early stage, rather than using information handling software. If your overlay program allows pictures to appear on-screen, these can be displayed on-screen rather than words. The record can be printed and displayed alongside the class weather chart. The benefit of the computer is that any number of days' weather can be stored easily.

## Activity 7

Three data collection sheets are provided on pages 56–58: 'Pets', 'Which Fruit Do You Like?' and 'Favourite Colours'. These introduce the children to collecting and recording other types of information. Children can ask questions of others in the class or group and colour, tick, cross or circle according to the response.

You may wish to enlarge the pictures so that children can have one to colour and then the pictures can be used to make a large class pictogram.

# Information Handling

## Activity 8

When the children have collected information on their sheet, or a class pictogram has been made, it is important to ask questions about the data. Such questions could include:

- How many?
- Which is the most/least?
- How many more?
- Which are the same?

You may wish to record children's responses to assess whether they have understood the activity and the information collected.

## Activity 9

There are many ways to link information handling with other areas of the curriculum to develop early geographical or historical enquiry, for example. The photocopiable sheet 'My Favourite Toy' (see page 60) is one example of a data collection sheet which can be used as part of a history topic on toys, old and new.

Ask each child to draw a picture of their favourite toy in the top section of the sheet. Help each child to write the name of their toy next to their picture. The child can then take the sheet home to ask their parent to draw a picture in the next box and name it, then a grandparent to draw a picture in the bottom box of a toy they used to play with.

The completed sheets can be cut up or photocopied and used for a class pictogram, or sorting activities. Comparisons can be made and discussions of changes over time. Other examples of this type of activity can include favourite places to play, where we go shopping, how we get to school.

## Activity 10

Later in school, the children will use database programs and CD-ROMs to search for specific information. Searching for information can be carried out in the early years' classroom by the teacher asking questions and setting tasks to find things from class collections. Your Nursery/Reception/P1 class may have made a collection and display of old and new toys. Children can be asked to find an old toy which needs to be pushed, or a new toy which works by battery.

## •• Vocabulary

Information, collect, store, sort, chart

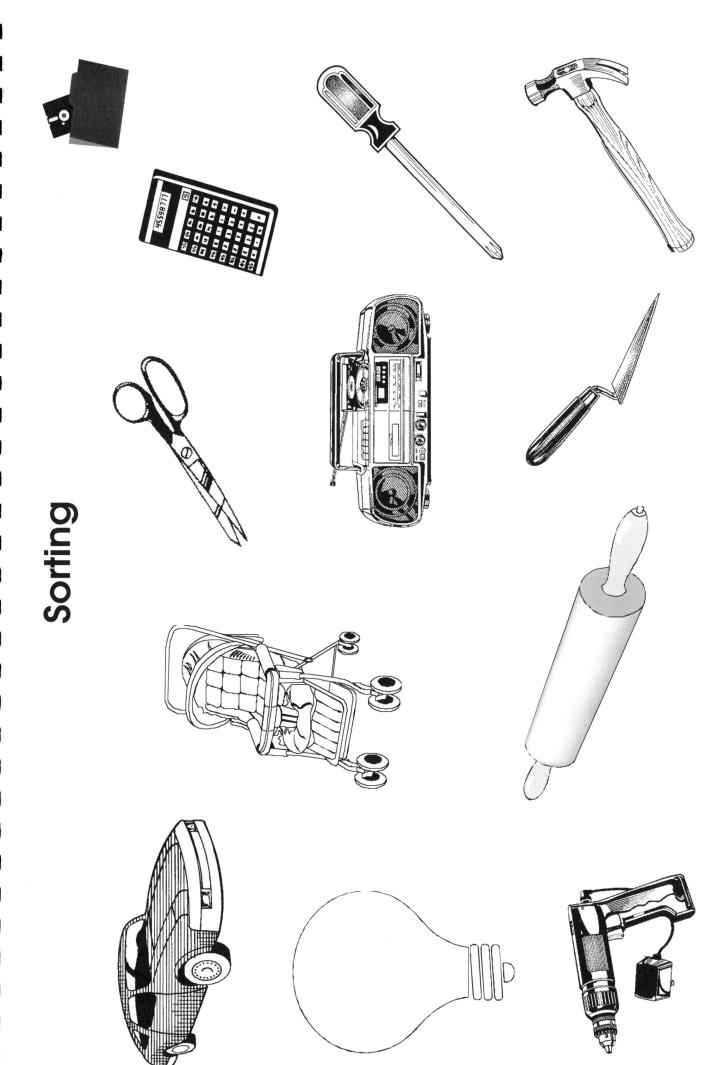

Information about _____

My name is _____

# What's the Weather Like?

# Pets

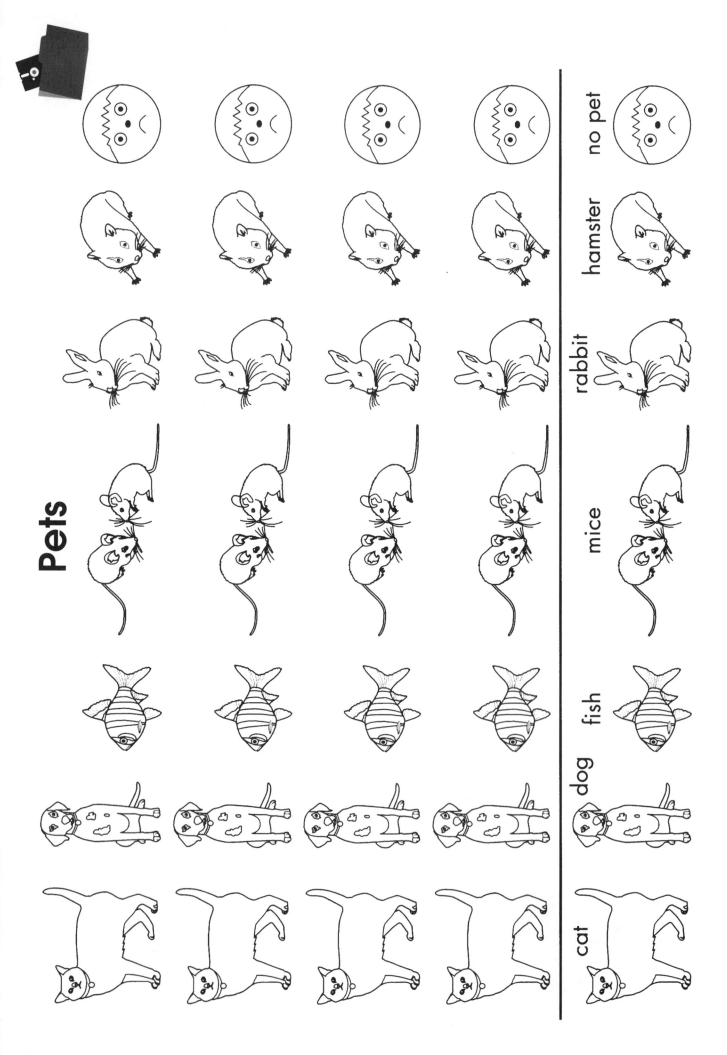

no pet

hamster

rabbit

mice

fish

dog

cat

# Which Fruit Do You Like?

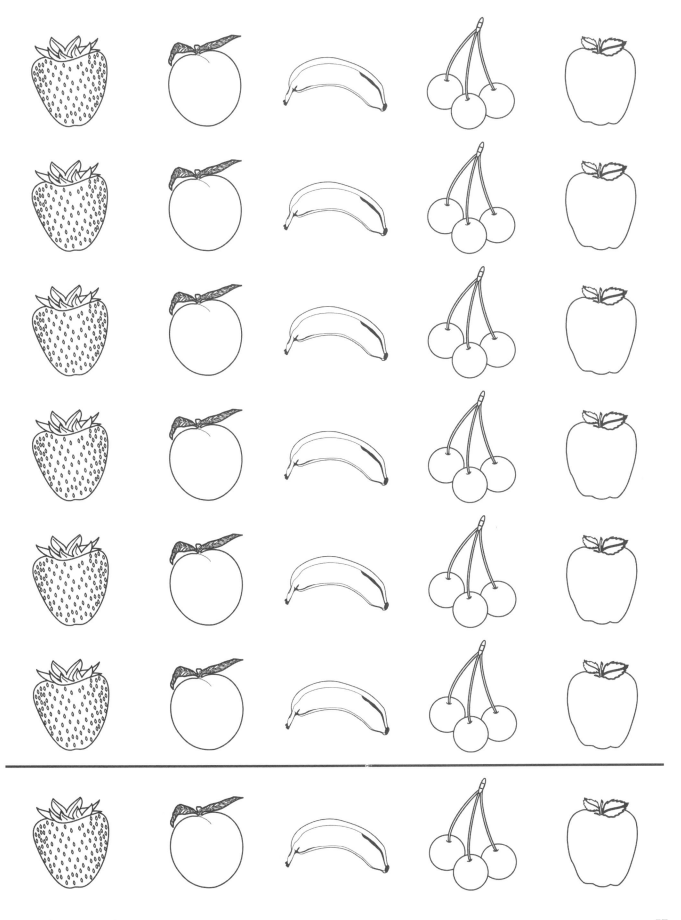

# Favourite Colours

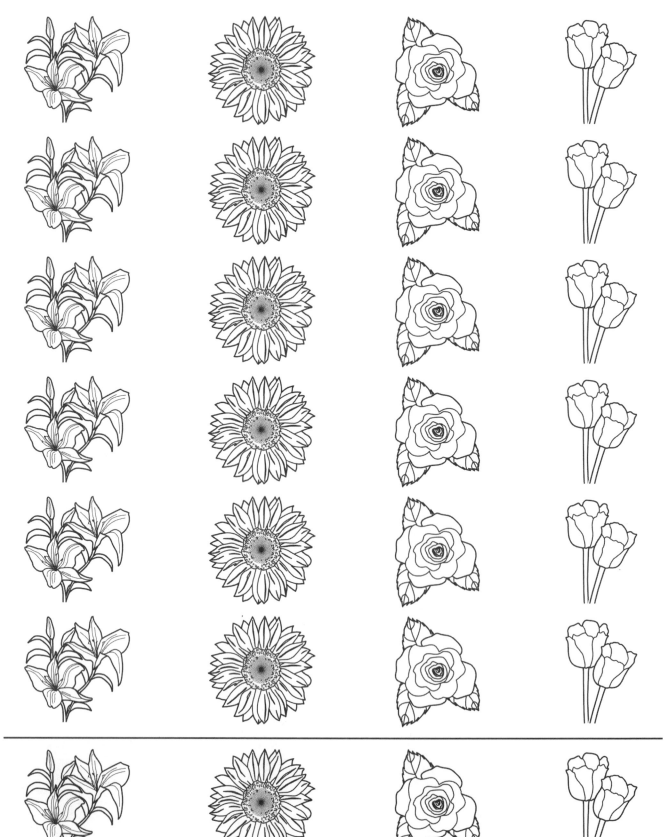

| blue | yellow | red | green |

# This Week's Weather

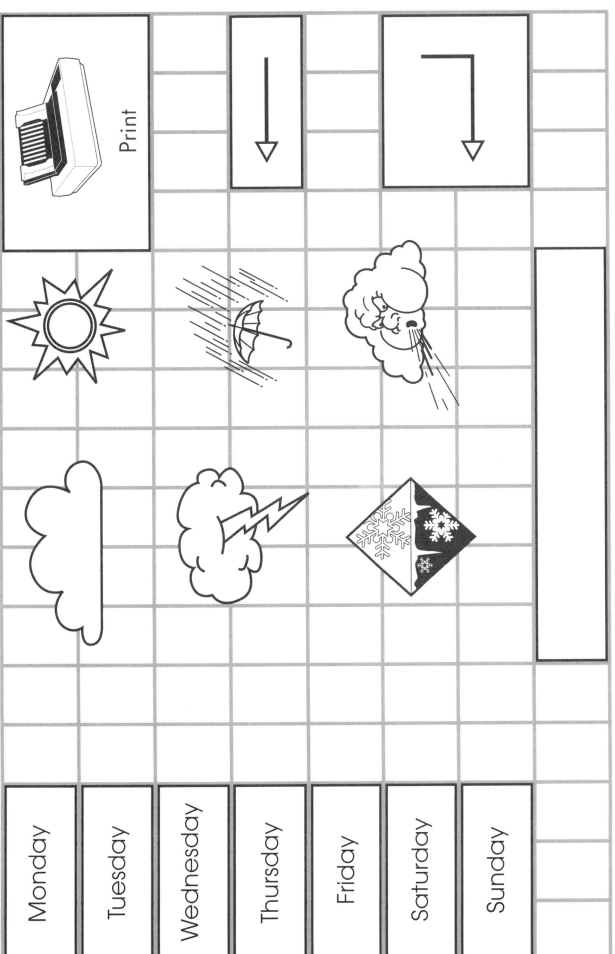

Print

| Monday | Tuesday | Wednesday | Thursday | Friday | Saturday | Sunday |
|--------|---------|-----------|----------|--------|----------|--------|

# My Favourite Toy

Me _____

# Skill Matrices

## General Technological Awareness

| Skill Activity | Skills Taught |
|---|---|
| 1 & 2 | • Understand what a computer is |
| 1 & 2 | • Identify the parts of a computer |
| 3 | • Explain the basics of how a computer operates |
| 3 | • Start, restart and shutdown a computer |
| 4, 5 & 6 | • Understand that appliances need to be switched on and off |
| 7 | • Understand the dos and don'ts of using a computer |
| 7 | • Demonstrate appropriate behaviour at the computer |
| 7 | • Treat equipment and disks with respect |
| 8 | • Identify a mouse and explain what it does |
| 9 | • Move a mouse and point it to a desired location |

## Paint, Draw and Graphics

| Skill Activity | Skills Taught |
|---|---|
| 1, 2, 3 & 5 | • Experiment with mouse control |
| 1, 2, 5 & 6 | • Experiment with colours |
| 1, 3, 4, 5, 6 & 7 | • Experiment with tools |

## Word Processing

| Skill Activity | Skills Taught |
|---|---|
| 1 & 2 | • Recognise lower case letters |
| 1 | • Match initial letters to pictures |
| 2, 3, 4 & 5 | • Match simple words to pictures |
| 4 & 6 | • Use an overlay keyboard to select lower case letters |
| 6 | • Recognise upper case letters |
| 6 | • Use an overlay keyboard with upper case and lower case |
| 6 | • Identify the space bar, return/enter key and delete/backspace key |

## Keyboarding

| Skill Activity | Skills Taught |
|---|---|
| 1, 2, 3, 4, 7 & 8 | • Recognise lower case letters |
| 1, 2, 5 & 6 | • Match initial letters to pictures |
| 5 & 6 | • Match simple words to pictures |
| 3, 4, 7, 8 & 9 | • Recognise upper case letters |
| 10 | • Use an overlay keyboard to select lower case letters |
| 10 & 11 | • Use an overlay keyboard with upper case and lower case |
| 12 | • Identify the space bar, return/enter key and delete/backspace key |

# Skill matrices

## Control

| Skill Activity | Skills Taught |
|---|---|
| 1, 2 & 3 | • Understand that control is an important aspect in everyday life |
| 2 | • Control devices purposefully by turning devices on and off |
| 4 & 5 | • Sequence instructions in order |
| 6, 7, 8 & 18 | • Understand forward and backward |
| 6, 7, 8 & 18 | • Understand left and right |
| 7 & 8 | • Experiment with turns |
| 6, 7, 8 & 9 | • Give separate commands to a partner to move |
| 8 & 9 | • Give a series of commands to a partner |
| 10, 12 & 13 | • Enter the forward command into a programmable toy (Roamer) |
| 10 | • Clear a command |
| 10, 15, 16 & 17 | • Use forward, CM and GO commands |
| 11, 15, 16 & 17 | • Use backward command |
| 14, 15, 16 & 17 | • Enter right and left turn commands |

## Video

| Skill Activity | Skills Taught |
|---|---|
| 1 | • Understand the function of a camcorder |
| 1 | • Locate the controls on a camcorder |
| 1 | • Switch the camera on and off |
| 1 | • Start and stop recording |
| 2 & 3 | • Use role-play to develop speaking skills |
| 2 & 3 | • Use role-play to develop social/co-operative skills |
| 2, 3, 4, 5, 6, 7, 8 & 9 | • Experiment with the use of a camcorder in the classroom |
| 4, 5, 6, 7, 8 & 9 | • Speak clearly to a camera |
| 4 & 9 | • Maintain eye contact with the camera |

## Information Handling

| Skill Activity | Skills Taught |
|---|---|
| 1 | • Understand that information can be stored |
| 4 | • Use role-play to simulate real life data handling |
| 1, 2, 3 & 10 | • Sort objects in the classroom in an order |
| 1, 2, 3 & 10 | • Classify or group a variety of objects |
| 2 | • Classify objects according to two criteria |
| 5 & 10 | • Search for and choose an object in response to a question |
| 5, 6, 10 | • Add a picture to a class pictogram |
| 8, 9, & 10 | • Answer simple questions about a pictogram |
| 5, 6, 7 & 9 | • Collect data |
| 5, 6, 7 & 9 | • Present data using a pictogram |

# Assessing I.C.T. Skills

## •• Checklist

It is important to keep a clear record of each child's progress through the I.C.T. activities. A record sheet is provided for this purpose. The aim of the record sheet is to provide an opportunity for assessment through the use of comments on each of the areas covered in Nursery/Reception/P1.

## •• Assessment

Combining record keeping and assessment is an excellent way to keep track of a child's progress. The comment box may be used by the child as a self-assessment of their own ability with the skills taught. This may be in conjunction with the teacher, who acts as a scribe at this early stage, using the school's existing record keeping system for an assessment comment. Alternatively, it can provide the opportunity for the teacher to write an assessment comment.

It is good practice to include a date with the comment for future reference. The use of the record sheet is flexible to fit in with existing record keeping and assessment systems within the school.

## •• Portfolio Assessment

One of the most effective means of child assessment is to organise individual portfolios of samples of a child's work. This allows the teacher, child and parents to understand quickly the progress made and the level of skills of the child.

## •• Recognising Achievement

It is important to include I.C.T. displays around the classroom, or I.C.T. work within existing displays in order to acknowledge the importance of using I.C.T. in everyday life.

Certificates of accomplishment for each section covered in Nursery/Reception/P1 are also provided in Co-ordinator's Manual 1 (Ages 4–7) to reward each child's performance. These can be integrated into the school's existing certificate/reward system

For more information about assessing I.C.T. skills, refer to the assessment section, Co-ordinator's Manual 1 (Ages 4–7).

# I.T. Works Record Sheet

## N/R/P1 CHECKLIST

Name _____

| General Technological Awareness | 1 | 2 | 3 | 4 | 5 | 6 | 7 | 8 | 9 | | | | | | | | | |
|---|---|---|---|---|---|---|---|---|---|---|---|---|---|---|---|---|---|---|
| Comment: | | | | | | | | | | | | | | | | | | |
| Paint, Draw and Graphics | 1 | 2 | 3 | 4 | 5 | 6 | 7 | | | | | | | | | | | |
| Comment: | | | | | | | | | | | | | | | | | | |
| Word Processing | 1 | 2 | 3 | 4 | 5 | 6 | | | | | | | | | | | | |
| Comment: | | | | | | | | | | | | | | | | | | |
| Keyboarding | 1 | 2 | 3 | 4 | 5 | 6 | 7 | 8 | 9 | 10 | 11 | 12 | | | | | | |
| Comment: | | | | | | | | | | | | | | | | | | |
| Control | 1 | 2 | 3 | 4 | 5 | 6 | 7 | 8 | 9 | 10 | 11 | 12 | 13 | 14 | 15 | 16 | 17 | 18 |
| Comment: | | | | | | | | | | | | | | | | | | |
| Video | 1 | 2 | 3 | 4 | 5 | 6 | 7 | 8 | 9 | | | | | | | | | |
| Comment: | | | | | | | | | | | | | | | | | | |
| Information Handling | 1 | 2 | 3 | 4 | 5 | 6 | 7 | 8 | 9 | 10 | | | | | | | | |
| Comment: | | | | | | | | | | | | | | | | | | |